DATE DUE

LOGGERHEAD TURTLE

Life Cycles

Jason Cooper

Rourke
Publishing LLC
Vero Beach, Florida 32964

www.rourkepublishing.com

PHOTO CREDITS: All photos © Lynn M. Stone

Cover: *A female loggerhead turtle has left the safety of the sea to nest on a Florida beach.*

Editor: Frank Sloan

Cover and page design by Nicola Stratford

Library of Congress Cataloging-in-Publication Data

Cooper, Jason, 1942-
  Loggerhead turtle / Jason Cooper.
      p. cm. — (Lifecycles)
Includes bibliographical references (p.   ).
  ISBN 1-58952-354-7 (hardcover)
  1. Loggerhead turtle—Juvenile literature. I. Title.
  QL666.C536 C65 2002
  597.92--dc21

                                                                    2002006230
Printed in the USA

MP/W

Table of Contents

A loggerhead turtle nests on Florida's Atlantic coast.

Crawling Ashore

Sea turtles spend almost their entire lives in the ocean. But the life cycle of the sea turtle begins on sandy beaches.

Each spring and summer female loggerhead sea turtles crawl on to the shore to lay eggs. They nest on beaches from New Jersey to Texas, but they are rarely seen north of North Carolina.

One Kind of Sea Turtle

The loggerhead is one of seven kinds of sea turtles. In the seas off America, however, nearly all sea turtles are loggerheads.

Crawling over sand is hard work for an animal that is made for life in the sea.

Loggerhead sea turtles nest at night, the coolest time of day.

A female loggerhead crawls ashore at night, when it is coolest. Still, dragging her 200-pound (91-kilogram) body with her flippers on sand is hard work.

People once thought that the liquid around a nesting sea turtle's eyes was tears from her labor.

Making a Nest

If nothing scares her, the female crawls onto the high beach where the sand is warmest. There she uses her hind flippers to scoop out a lightbulb-shaped nest hole. She lays about 100 eggs into the nest. While she nests, her eyes drip to remove body salt and wash away sand. The turtle isn't crying from her nesting effort.

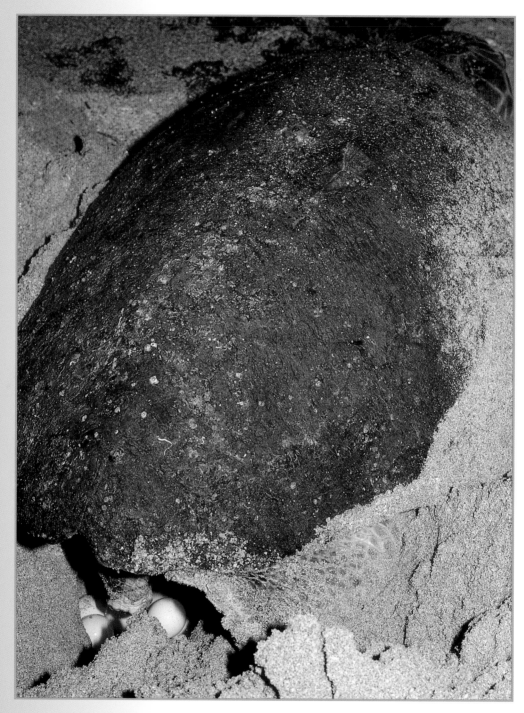

Female loggerheads may nest several times in a single year.

A loggerhead may nest as many as seven times during a nesting season. Each nesting is about 12 days apart. One loggerhead that nested six times in Florida laid 920 eggs.

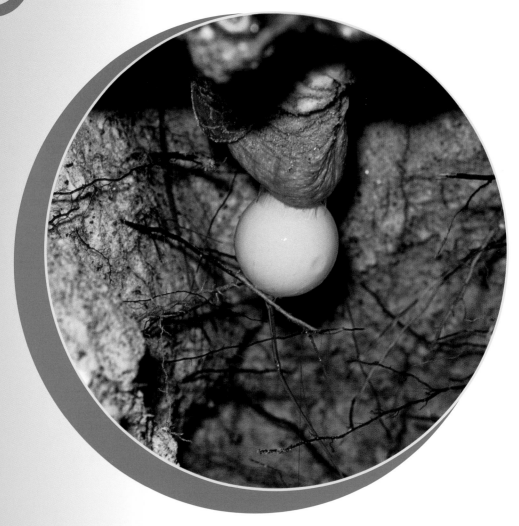

A loggerhead lays an egg into a nest hole.

After laying eggs, the turtle fills the nest hole with sand. Again, she uses her hind flippers like little shovels.

Leaving the Nest Behind

Like most **reptiles**, the loggerhead lays eggs and then leaves them. A female loggerhead is a mother only for the hour or so that she's on the beach. Male loggerheads almost never come ashore for any reason.

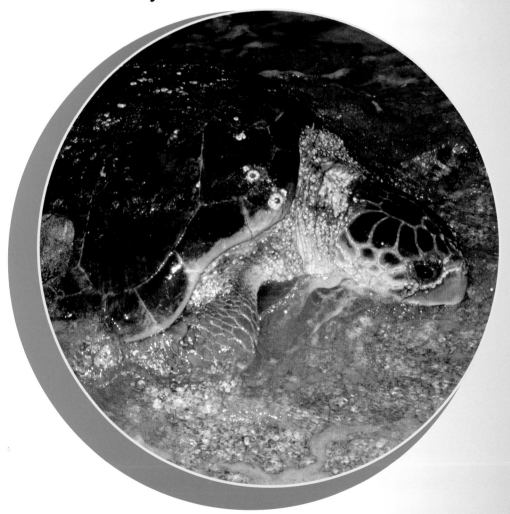

After laying about 100 eggs, this mother loggerhead returns to her home at sea.

Hatching loggerhead babies almost explode from their sandy nest.

Hatchlings

The eggs remain in the sand for 50 to 60 days. During that time, the bodies of the little turtles develop in the eggs. After that period of **incubation**, the turtles are ready to hatch. Perhaps one in 1,000 will live to become adults in about 30 years.

At the nest, tiny, gray heads poke up through the sand. Then more heads and flippers appear. Soon the tiny **hatchlings** burst from the sand.

Hatchlings rush to the sea on an August night.

Rush to the Sea

The baby turtles rush toward the sea. It's a short but dangerous journey. Hatchlings are bite-size snacks for raccoons and night **herons**.

Once into the sea, the hatchlings may be **prey** for big fish. The turtles that survive swim into huge, floating mats of seaweed. There they can grow and hide for several years.

Growing Up

The little turtles eat tiny plants and animals. As they grow larger, they become true **predators**. They eat an all-meat diet of sponges, shellfish, and jellyfish.

Young loggerheads switch from a diet of small creatures to shellfish and other, larger ocean creatures.

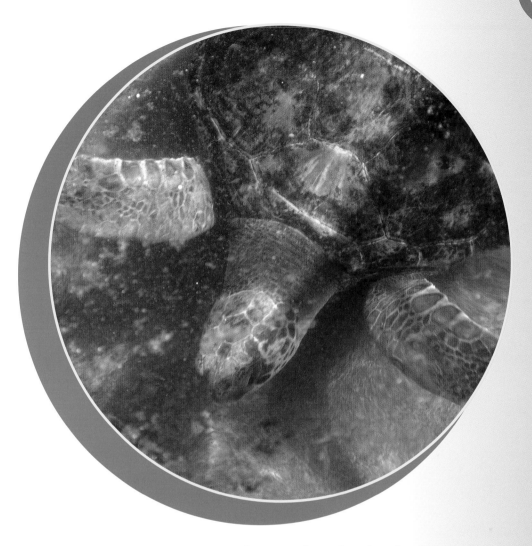

Loggerheads at sea travel many hundreds of miles.

Adult loggerheads travel many hundreds of miles. Their travel takes them to places where food is plentiful.

Children watch a loggerhead nesting on a Florida beach.

The Life Cycle Goes On

One day their travel takes them "home." Sea turtles return to nest on the same beach where they were born. There a new **generation** of loggerheads begins.

How does a turtle at sea find one particular beach hundreds of miles away? Scientists would like to know, too. But for now it remains a mystery.

Stage 1: Loggerheads leave the sea to lay eggs in nests on beaches during spring and summer.

Stage 4: When they are fully grown, loggerheads return to lay their eggs on the same beach where they were born.

Stage 2: Buried in the sand, the eggs hatch after 50 to 60 days.

Stage 3: After they hatch, the small turtles head for the sea.

Glossary

generation (jen er AY shun) — a group of individuals born and living at the same time

hatchlings (HATCH lingz) — newly hatched individuals

herons (HAIR unz) — any of several kinds of wading birds with long legs and long, sharp beaks

incubation (INK you bay shun) — keeping eggs warm; developing and growing within an egg

predators (PRED uh terz) — animals that catch and eat other animals for food

prey (PRAY) — an animal that is eaten by another animal

reptiles (REP tilez) — any one of the group of cold-blooded animals with scales, including alligators, crocodiles, turtles, snakes, and the tuatara

Index

Further Reading

Lepthien, Emile. *Sea Turtles.* Children's Press, 1996
Staub, Frank. *Sea Turtles.* Lerner, 1994

Websites to Visit

http://www.cccturtle.org/
http://search.yahooligans.com/search/ligans?p=loggerhead+turtle

About the Author

Jason Cooper has written several children's books about a variety of topics for Rourke Publishing, including recent series *China Discovery* and *American Landmarks*. Cooper travels widely to gather information for his books. Two of his favorite travel destinations are Alaska and the Far East.